William Bolcom

I Will Breathe a Mountain

A Song Cycle
from American Women Poets

This work was commissioned for Marilyn Horne by the Carnegie Hall Corporation in honor of Carnegie Hall's centennial season. The world premiere was given at Carnegie Hall, New York City, on March 26, 1991.

ISBN 0-7935-4239-1

EXCLUSIVELY DISTRIBUTED BY

EDWARD B. MARKS MUSIC COMPANY / HAL•LEONARD CORPORATION

7777 W. BLUEMOUND RD. P.O. BOX 13819 MILWAUKEE, WI 53213

Composer's Note

Marilyn Horne requested a cycle made up of poems by American women. I felt that, although I could have put together an anthology myself, the cycle would have a very strong profile if the selections were made with the aid of an American woman poet, and I accordingly asked my friend Alice Fulton for help; she then gave me a list of around 30 poems. Marilyn Horne then told me which of those she liked, I added those I liked, and that is how the selection was made.

William Bolcom

Note: Accidentals apply throughout a beamed note-group; they are repeated within a measure otherwise:

In music with key-signature, traditional rules apply.

Contents

1. Pity Me Not Because the Light of Day

Edna St. Vincent Millay

William Bolcom

thick - et as the year goes by; Pit-y me not the wan-ing of the

moon, Nor that the eb - bing tide goes out to sea, Nor that a man's de - sire ____ is hushed so

soon, And you no long-er look with love on me. ____

This have I known al - ways: Love is no more than the wide blos-som which the wind as-sails,

Than the great tide that treads the shift-ing   shore ___ strew-ing   fresh wreck-age   gath-ered in the

gales:

that the   heart   is   slow   to   learn   What the swift

mind be-holds ___   at ev'-ry   turn.

as at first

a piacere

a tempo

Pit-y me ___

June 16, 1990
Ann Arbor, MI
ca. 2:45

2. How To Swing Those Obbligatos Around

Alice Fulton

William Bolcom

(*) Grace-notes, rolled chords, and the like come before the beat.

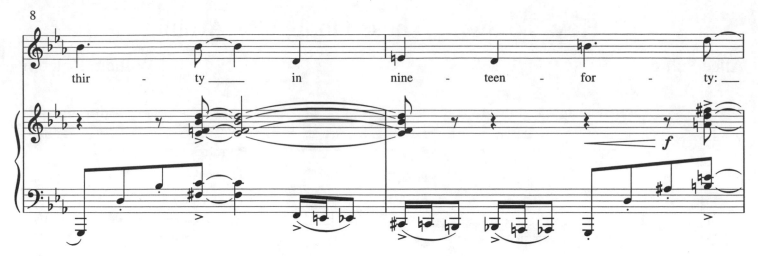

thir - ty _____ in nine - teen - for - ty: _____

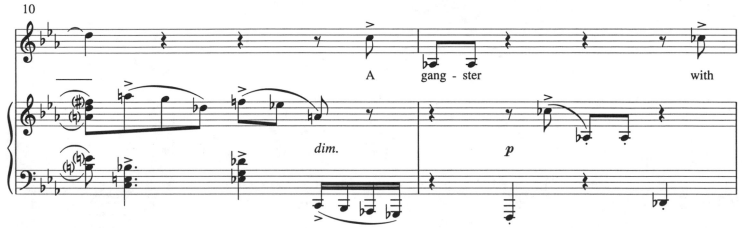

A gang - ster with

pa - tent leath - er shoes to shine un - der girls' skirts _____ & a moth - er who called him

son - ny. He should have crashed a club _____ where they

ca - tered to the smart set, dis - pos - ing of the bounc - er with

mf , spoken, cool

You spent three months in a plas - ter cast the last time you tan - gled with me

& I should have been the sing - er in tight cham - pagne

— skin _____ wait - ing for him to growl. I don't

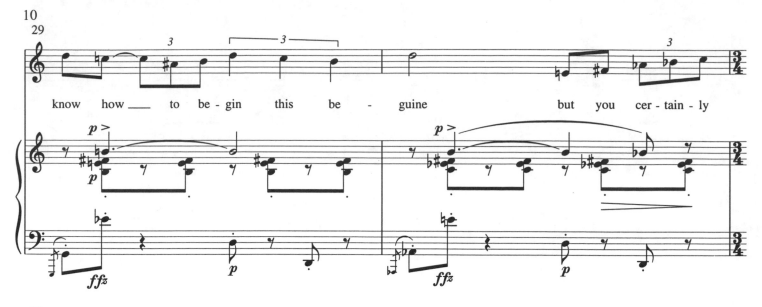

know how ___ to be - gin this be - guine but you cer - tain - ly

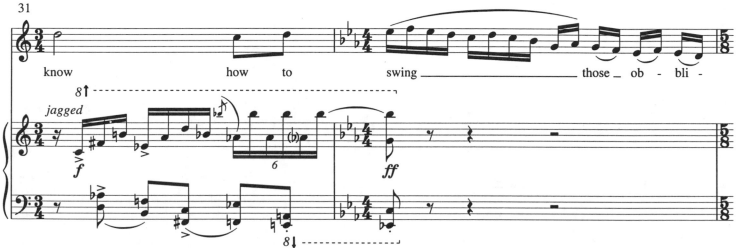

know how to swing ___ those _ ob - bli -

ga - tos a - round, how to swing ___ those _ ob - bli -

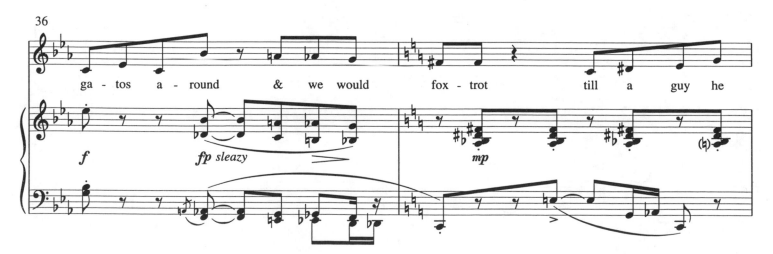

ga - tos a - round & we would fox - trot till a guy he

38

rit. _ _ _ _ _

p

knew from Sing__ Sing cut in. _____ & he

a tempo

41

f

said he loved old flicks I should come up to his

fz

dry

44

place & see the art de - co ash - trays__ on his

p ominous

mp

46

freely in tempo

shag rug that I should - n't waste my - self at

p *f* *p* *cresc.*

Bell tel but mar-ry him & take his

bus - iness calls & I said

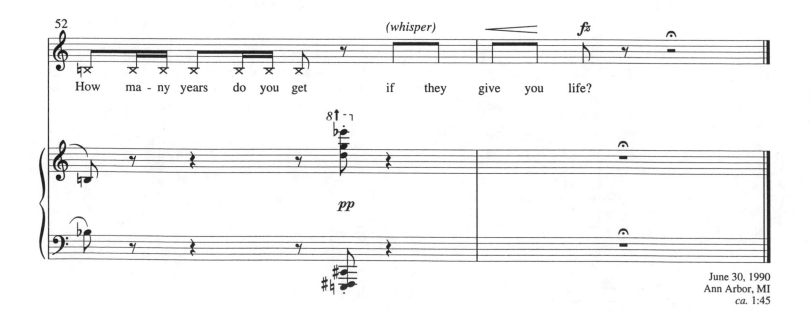

How ma - ny years do you get if they give you life?

June 30, 1990
Ann Arbor, MI
ca. 1:45

3. The Crazy Woman

Gwendolyn Brooks

William Bolcom

15

July 14, 1990
Ann Arbor, MI
ca. 2:15"

(*) Accent B♭ in l.h. thumb, then hold after last chord; hold B♭ with S.P. into next song after 🎶 is released.

4. Just Once

Anne Sexton

William Bolcom

N.B. Voice: If songs are in sequence, get B♭ from previous song (see page 12).

walked there a - long the Charles Ri - ver, watched the lights

co - py - ing them - selves, _____ all ne - oned and strobe - heart - ed,

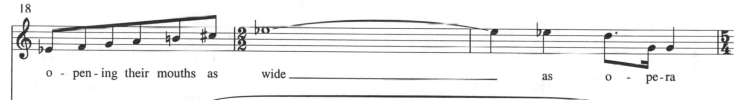

o - pen - ing their mouths as wide _____ as o - pe - ra

sing - ers; coun - ted the stars, my lit - tle cam - paign - ers,

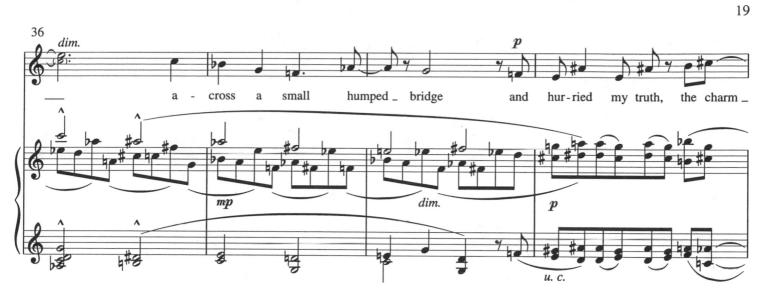

a - cross a small humped _ bridge and hur - ried my truth, the charm _

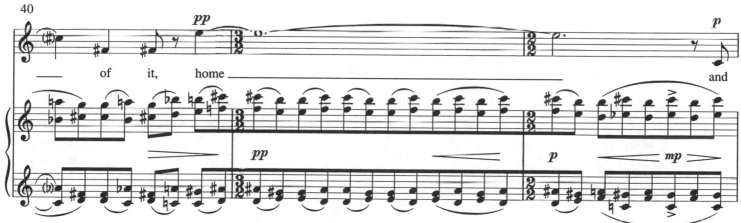

_ of it, home _____ and

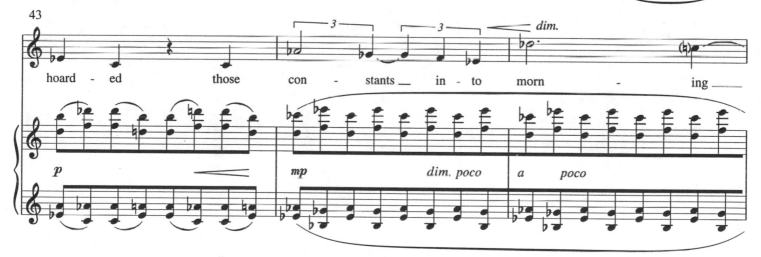

hoard - ed those con - stants _ in - to morn - ing ____

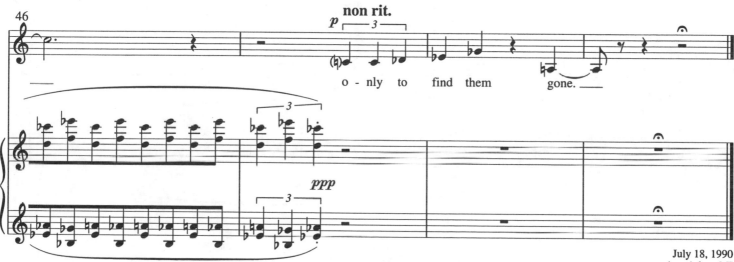

o - nly to find them gone. ____

July 18, 1990
Ann Arbor, MI
ca. 1:20

5. Never More Will the Wind

H.D. (pen name for Hilda Doolittle)

William Bolcom

October 23, 1989
Ann Arbor, MI
(rev. July 15, 1990)
ca. 2:00

6. The Sage

Denise Levertov

William Bolcom

knows. Sweep the rose - meat up, throw the

bits out in the rain. He

nev - er eats ev-ery crumb, says the hearts are bit - ter. That's the way he

is, he knows the world and the wea - ther.

May 9, 1990
New York City
ca. 1:22

7. O To Be A Dragon

Marianne Moore

William Bolcom

June 11, 1990
Ann Arbor, MI
ca. 1:00

8. The Bustle in a House

Emily Dickinson

William Bolcom

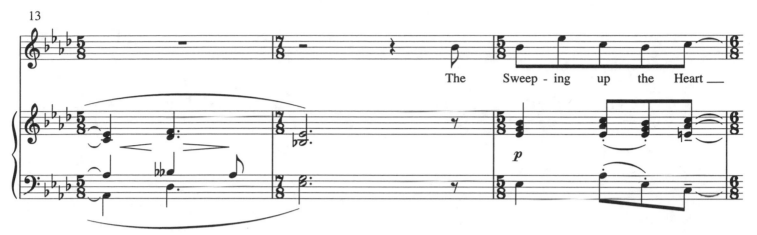

The Sweep-ing up the Heart

And put-ting Love a-way ___ We

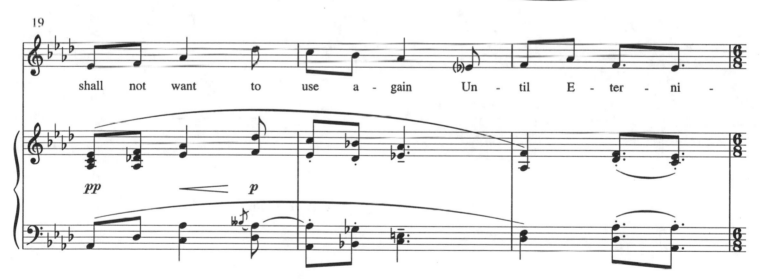

shall not want to use a-gain Un - til E - ter - ni -

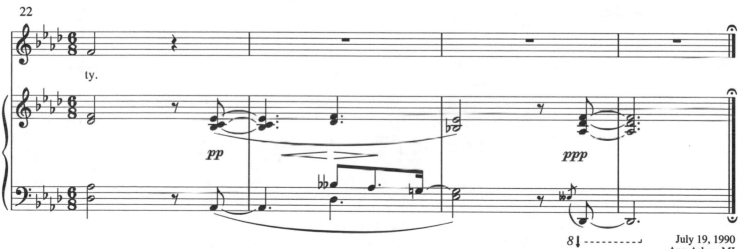

ty.

July 19, 1990
Ann Arbor, MI
ca. 2:00

9. I Saw Eternity

Louise Bogan

William Bolcom

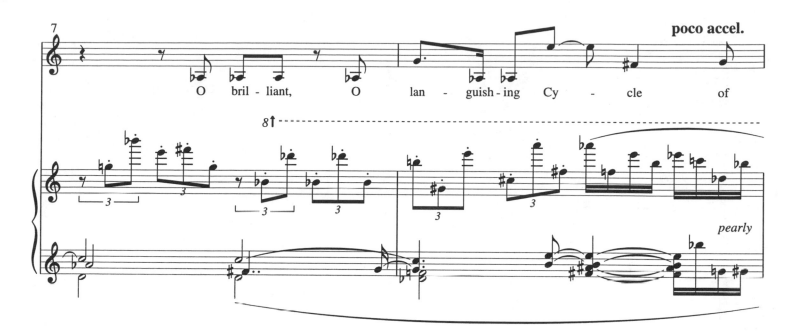

Here's a crumb ____ of For - ev - er!

July 26, 1990
Ann Arbor, MI
ca. 1:30

10. Night Practice

May Swenson

William Bolcom

Stately, tranquil; with strength. Very steady.

In quarter-notes, c. ♩ = 80

sucked-in breath a val - ley, _____ with my pushed-out breath a moun - tain. _____

I will make a val - ley

wid - er than the whis - per, I will make a high - er

moun - tain than the cry; _____ will with my will breathe a

June 9, 1990
Ann Arbor, MI
ca. 2:50

attacca

11. The Fish

Elizabeth Bishop

William Bolcom

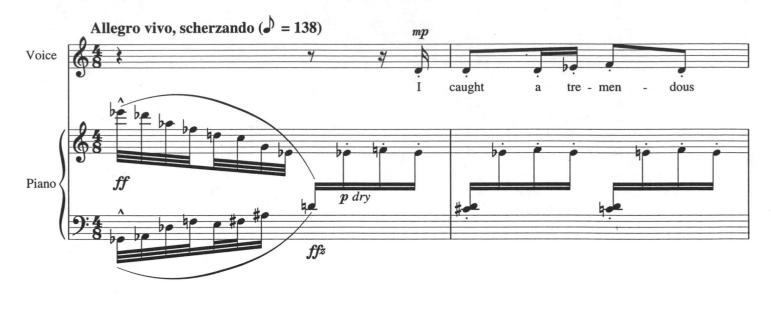

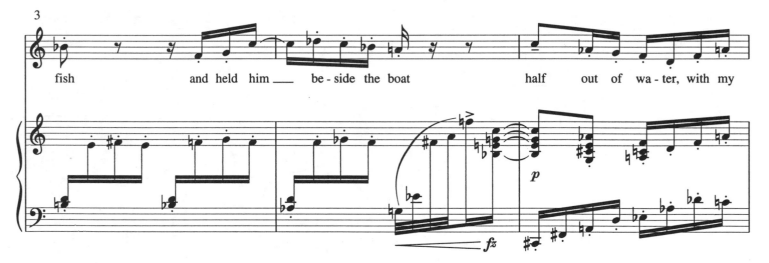

N.B. This poem is slightly abridged from the original.

"The Fish" from **The Complete Poems 1927 - 1979** by Elizabeth Bishop.
Copyright © 1940, 1968 by Elizabeth Bishop. Used by arrangement with Farrar, Straus & Giroux, Inc.

fight. He had-n't fought at all. ___ He hung a grunt-ing weight,

bat-tered and ve-ne-ra - ble and home - ly.

Here and there his brown skin hung in

strips like an - cient wall - pa - per, and its pat - tern of

down. _____ While his gills were breath - ing

in the ter - ri - ble ox - y- gen the fright - en - ing

gills, fresh and crisp with blood, that can cut so

bad - ly _____ I

* Ossia: f

While his gills were breath - ing in the ter - ri - ble ox - y- gen

saw   that from his lo - wer lip   if you could call it a lip

grim, ___ wet, and weap-on-like,   hung five old pie - ces of

fish - line,   with all their five big hooks grown firm - ly in his

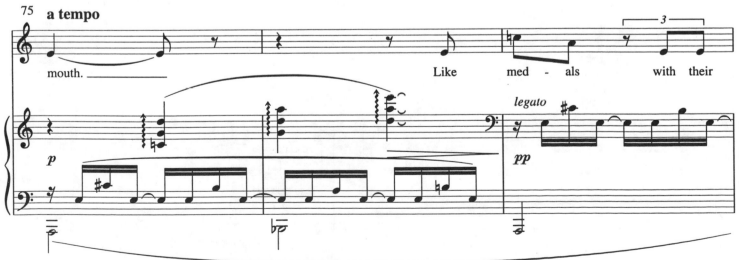

mouth. _____   Like med - als with their

 rib - bons frayed and wa - ver-ing, a

five - haired beard of wis - dom

trail - ing from his ach - ing jaw. _____

gossamer Ped.

I stared and stared and

October 23, 1989
rev. July 15, 1990
Ann Arbor, MI
ca. 3:20

Texts of the poetry of
"I Will Breathe a Mountain"

Pity Me Not Because the Light of Day

EDNA ST. VINCENT MILLAY

Pity me not because the light of day
At close of day no longer walks the sky;
Pity me not for beauties passed away
From field and thicket as the year goes by;
Pity me not the waning of the moon,
Nor that a man's desire is hushed so soon,
And you no longer look with love on me.
This have I known always:
Love is no more
Than the wide blossom which the
    wind assails,
Than the great tide that treads
    the shifting shore,
Strewing fresh wreckage gathered
    in the gales:
Pity me that the heart is slow to learn
What the swift mind beholds
    at every turn.

How To Swing Those Obbligatos Around

ALICE FULTON

He had shag hair & a boutique.
In the bar he told me I had too much class
to be a telephone operator & I told him
he should have been thirty in 1940:
a gangster with patent leather shoes
to shine under girl's skirts & a mother
who called him sonny. He should have
crashed a club where they catered
to the smart set, disposing of
the bouncer with You spent three months
in a plaster cast the last time
you tangled with me & I should have been
the singer in tight champagne
skin waiting for him to growl
I don't know how to begin
this beguine but you certainly know how to
swing those obbligatos around & we
would fox-trot till a guy
he knew from Sing Sing cut in.
& he said he loved old flicks
I should come up to his place & see
the art deco ashtrays on his shag rug
that I shouldn't waste myself
at Bell tel but marry him
& take his business calls &
I said How many years do you get
if they give you life

The Crazy Woman

GWENDOLYN BROOKS

I shall not sing a May song.
A May song should be gay.
I'll wait until November
And sing a song of gray.

I'll wait until November.
That is the time for me.

I'll go out in the frosty dark
And sing most terribly.

And all the little people
Will stare at me and say,
"That is the Crazy Woman
Who would not sing in May."

Just Once

ANNE SEXTON

Just once I knew what life was for.
In Boston, quite suddenly, I understood;
walked there along the Charles River,
watched the lights copying themselves,
all neoned and strobe-hearted, opening
their mouths as wide as opera singers;
counted the stars, my little campaigners,
my scar daisies, and knew that I walked
my love
on the night green side of it and cried
my heart to the eastbound cars and cried
my heart to the westbound cars and took
my truth across a small humped bridge
and hurried my truth, the charm
    of it, home
and hoarded these constants into morning
only to find them gone.

Never More Will The Wind

H.D.

Never more will the wind
cherish you again,
never more will the rain.

Never more
shall we find you bright
in the snow and wind.

The snow is melted,
the snow is gone,
and you are flown:

Like a bird out of our hand,
like a light out of our heart,
you are gone.

The Sage

DENISE LEVERTOV

The cat is eating the roses:
that's the way he is.
Don't stop him, don't stop
the world going round,
that's the way things are.
The third of May
was misty; fourth of May
who knows. Sweep

the rose-meat up, throw the bits
out in the rain.
He never eats
every crumb, says
the hearts are bitter.
That's the way he is, he knows
the world and the weather.

O To Be A Dragon

MARIANNE MOORE

If I, like Solomon,...
could have my wish—

my wish...O to be a dragon,
a symbol of the power of Heaven—

of silkworm
size or immense; at times invisible.
Felicitous phenomenon!

The Bustle In a House

EMILY DICKINSON

The Bustle in a House
The Morning after Death
Is solemnest of industries
Enacted Upon Earth—

The Sweeping up the Heart
And putting Love away
We shall not want to use again
Until Eternity.

I Saw Eternity

LOUISE BOGAN

O beautiful Forever!
O grandiose Everlasting!
Now, now, now,
I break you into pieces,
I feed you to the ground.
O brilliant, O languishing
Cycle of weeping light!
The mice and birds will eat you,
And you will spoil their stomachs
As you have spoiled my mind.

Here, mice, rats,
Porcupines and toads,
Moles, shrews, squirrels,
Weasels, turtles, lizards,—
Here's bright Everlasting!
Here's a crumb of Forever!
Here's a crumb of Forever!

Night Practice

MAY SWENSON

I
will
remember
with my breath
to make a mountain,
with my sucked-in breath
a valley, with my pushed-out
breath a mountain. I will make
a valley wider than the whisper, I
will make a higher mountain than the cry;
will with my will breathe a mountain, I will
with my will breathe a valley. I will push out
a mountain, suck in a valley, deeper than the shout
YOU MUST DIE, harder, heavier, sharper a mountain than
the truth YOU MUST DIE. I will remember. My breath will
make a mountain. My will will remember to will. I, suck-
ing, pushing, I will breathe a valley, I will breathe a mountain.

—"Night Practice" by May Swenson. Copyright 1963 by May Swenson.
Used with permission of The Literary Estate of May Swenson

The Fish

ELIZABETH BISHOP

I caught a tremendous fish
and held him beside the boat
half out of water, with my hook
fast in a corner of his mouth.
He didn't fight.
He hadn't fought at all.
He hung a grunting weight,
battered and venerable
and homely. Here and there
his brown skin hung in strips
like ancient wallpaper,
and its pattern of darker brown
was like wallpaper:
shapes like full-blown roses
stained and lost through age.
He was speckled with barnacles,
fine rosettes of lime,
and infested
with tiny white sea-lice,
and underneath two or three
rags of green weed hung down.
While his gills were breathing in
the terrible oxygen
—the frightening gills,
fresh and crisp with blood,
that can cut so badly—
I thought of the coarse white flesh
packed in like feathers,
the big bones and the little bones,
the dramatic reds and blacks
of his shiny entrails,
and the pink swim-bladder
like a big peony.
I looked into his eyes
which were far larger than mine
but shallower, and yellowed,
the irises backed and packed
with tarnished tinfoil
seen through the lenses
of old scratched isinglass.
They shifted a little, but not
to return my stare.
—It was more like the tipping
of an object toward the light.
I admired his sullen face,
the mechanism of his jaw,
and then I saw
that from his lower lip
—if you could call it a lip—
grim, wet, and weaponlike,
hung five old pieces of fish-line,
or four and a wire leader
with the swivel still attached,
with all their five big hooks
grown firmly in his mouth.
A green line, frayed at the end
where he broke it, two heavier lines,
and a fine black thread
still crimped from the strain and snap
when it broke and he got away.
Like medals with their ribbons
frayed and wavering,
a five-haired beard of wisdom
trailing from his aching jaw.
I stared and stared
and victory filled up
the little rented boat,
from the pool of bilge
where oil had spread a rainbow
around the rusted engine
to the bailer rusted orange,
the sun-cracked thwarts,
the oarlocks on their strings,
the gunnels—until everything
was rainbow, rainbow, rainbow!
And I let the fish go.

—"The Fish" from The Complete Poems, 1927-1979 by Elizabeth Bishop.
Copyright 1940, 1968 by Elizabeth Bishop.
Used by arrangement with Farrar, Straus and Giroux, Inc.